GIAN CARLO
MENOTTI

AMAHL AND THE NIGHT VISITORS

Opera in One Act

(piano-vocal score)

words and music by
Gian Carlo Menotti

1997 Edition

ED 2039

ISBN 978-0-88188-965-9

G. SCHIRMER, Inc.

DISTRIBUTED BY

HAL•LEONARD®
CORPORATION
7777 W. BLUEMOUND RD. P.O. BOX 13819 MILWAUKEE, WI 53213

Amahl and the Night Visitors is the first opera commissioned especially for television, and was given its premiere by the NBC Television Opera Theatre in New York City on December 24, 1951. The following cast took part in this performance:

Amahl . . . . Chet Allen
His Mother . . . . Rosemary Kuhlmann
King Kaspar . . . . Andrew McKinley
King Melchior . . . . David Aiken
King Balthazar . . . . Leon Lishner
The Page . . . . Francis Monachino

Thomas Schippers, Conductor

The entire production was staged by Mr. Menotti. The settings and costumes were designed by Eugene Berman. John Butler designed the choreography. Serving for NBC Television were Samuel Chotzinoff, producer; Charles Polachek, associate producer; Kirk Browning, television director; and George Voutsas, audio director.

The first professional production was given on April 9, 1952 by the New York City Opera.

Current Recordings on CD

Soloists, NBC Symphony Orchestra and Chorus, cond. Thomas Schippers
RCA Victor, 6485–2–RG

Soloists, Royal Opera House Orchestra and Chorus, cond. David Syrus
That's Entertainment Records, CDTER 1124

Orchestral excerpts (*Introduction, March and Shepherds' Dance*)
New Zealand Symphony, cond. Andrew Schenck
Koch International Classics, 3–7005–2

In 1997 a film version was made in Spoleto, Italy, under the composer's supervision.

CHARACTERS

Amahl (a crippled boy of about 12) . . . . Boy Soprano
His Mother . . . . Soprano
King Kaspar (slightly deaf) . . . . Tenor
King Melchior . . . . Baritone
King Balthazar . . . . Bass
The Page . . . . Bass

Chorus of Shepherds and Villagers
Dancers

INSTRUMENTATION

Flute (doubling Piccolo)
2 Oboes
Clarinet in B♭ (doubling Clarinet in A)
Bassoon

Horn in F
Trumpet in C

Percussion (2 players):
    Timpani, Triangle, Tambourine,
    Suspended Cymbal, Snare Drum

Piano
Harp

Strings

A orchestra score is available for purchase (order no. 50340770).

Performance material is available on rental.

PRODUCTION NOTES

The Setting

The stage is divided into two areas. One is the interior of the shepherd's hut where Amahl and his mother live. At the extreme right is a low bench, built against the wall, which serves as the Mother's bed and later as the seat to which the Kings are ushered. The bench is covered with straw and sheepskins. Up center is the fireplace, low, rounded, made of stone. Left of the fireplace is a pallet of straw, Amahl's bed. There are few objects in the room. Beside the fireplace is a low, rough-hewn stool. On the mantel there is a small oil lamp, which throws a meager light into the room. In the corner above Amahl's bed hangs a birdcage made of twisted vines. Except for a few peasant's implements, the room is otherwise bare, clean-swept. The wood and the stone of the hut have aged and weathered into the hues of grey, brown and green which bespeak poverty.

The third wall of the hut, containing the door and the window, divides the stage, with the door downstage. The door is heavy, wooden, held on a large wooden latch. The window is broken into crudely-fashioned panes, divides at the center, and pushes outward. Near the door, on the outside, is a large stone.

Surrounding the hut is the countryside, strewn with little hamlets perched precariously among the distant hills. Past the door of the hut goes the road. The road turns down and out of sight at the extreme left, to reappear winding through the hills. Snow lies softly on the ground. The night sky is pierced by many stars, but the Star of the East with its flaming tail floods both sky and earth with a glowing radiance.

The Costumes

Amahl, the Mother, and the Shepherds are clothed in the plainest homespun materials. Leg bindings, hats fashioned from straw and reeds, rough-cut cloaks, all are the marks of the shepherd's trade. The costumes should suggest the anachronistic character of those figures one sees in a Neapolitan *presepio*, or in any of the paintings of the Flemish and Italian primitives.

The Three Kings are magnificently clad, fulfilling in the richness of their dress, their jewels and their robes a child's most colorful dream of what an Orient King should wear. King Melchior carries the coffer of gold, symbol of power, King Balthazar the urn of incense, symbol of prayer, and King Kaspar the chalice of myrrh, symbol of death. The Page is costumed as an oriental slave. The bundles he carries are wrapped richly in furs and cloth of gold. Both King Balthazar and the Page are Nubian.

The Characters and the Action

Amahl, a child, is the focal figure of the opera.* Hence, all the action, and even the characterization of the adult figures, is dictated by his point of view. The seeming severity of the Mother, the occasionally colloquial conduct of the Three Kings, the visit of the Shepherds, the theft of the gold, and the miracle—all these must be interpreted simply and directly in terms of a child's imagination.

---

* It is the express wish of the composer that the role of Amahl should always be performed by a boy. Neither the musical nor the dramatic concept of the opera permits the substitution of a woman costumed as a child.

AMAHL AND THE NIGHT VISITORS

Words and Music by
Gian Carlo Menotti

(The curtain rises. It is night. The crystal-clear winter sky is dotted with stars, the Eastern Star flaming a -
mongst them. Outside the cottage, not far from its door, Amahl, wrapped in an oversized cloak, sits on a stone,
playing his shepherd's pipe. His crudely-made crutch lies on the ground beside him. Within, the Mother works at
household chores. The room is lighted only by the dying fire and the low flame of a tiny oil lamp.)

2

4

Amahl: moon has-n't ris-en yet, let me stay a lit-tle...

Mother: *(clapping her hands)* There won't be an-y moon t

Amahl: Oh, ver-y wel

Mother: *liberamente* night. But there will be__ a weep-ing child ver-y soon, if he does-n't hur-ry up and o-bey his moth-er.
(The Mother closes the wind with a sharp little bang.)

(Reluctantly, Amahl rises, takes up his crutch, and hobbles into the house. On the pegs to one

of the door he hangs his heavy cloak and shepherd's cap. His pipe he places carefully in the corner. The Mother kn at the fireplace, trying to coax a flame from the few remaining twigs. Amahl returns to the open door and le against it, looking up to the sk

6

8

Mother: And if that were-n't e-nough, the star has a tail and the tail is of fire!

⑮ *a tempo*

p

(103)

liberamente

(Amahl measures the air as wide as his arms can reach.)

(At her frown, he reduc the size by half.)

Amahl: But there is a star and it has a tail this long.

Well... may-be on-ly...

pp

105

a tempo

Amahl: this long. But it's there! Cross my heart and hope to die.

(clasping Amahl in her arms)

Mother: A - mahl!

⑯ *a tempo*

Poor A - mahl!—

p secco

f

(106)

Mother: Hun - ger has gone to your head. Dear God, what is a poor wid - ow to do,—

109

(She moves disconsolately to the fireplace.)

molto meno mosso

when her cup-boards and pock-ets are emp-ty and ev-'ry-thing sold? Un-less we go beg-ging

how shall we live through to-mor-row? My lit-tle son, a beg-gar!

(She sinks, weeping, onto a little stool.)

(Amahl goes to her and embraces her tenderly, stroking her hair.)

Amahl

Andante calmo

Don't cry, Moth-er dear, don't wor-ry for me. If we must go beg-ging, a good

beg-gar I'll be. I know sweet tunes to set peo-ple danc-ing. We'll

walk and walk from vil-lage to town, you dressed as a gyp-sy and I as a clown. We'll

noon we shall eat roast goose and sweet al - monds, at night we shall sleep w.

My dream - er, good night! You're wast - ing the light.

sheep and the stars. Good night.

Kiss me good night. Good night.

(The Mother rises and bends
to receive the good-night kiss.)

(Amahl goes to his pallet of straw at one side of the fireplace. The Mother secures the door, takes

②④ Allegro, con moto

Amahl's cloak and spreads it over him, touches his head tenderly, then, having snuffed out the tiny oil lamp, she lies
down on the bench. The lights die from the room except for a faint glow in the fireplace and the radiance of the sky
through the window.)

*This effect can be achieved by using either puppets or children, costumed exactly like the adult figures.

Allegro *(Amahl goes to the door and opens it a crack.)*

(He quickly closes the door, and runs to his mother.)

Amahl

poco più agitato

Moth-er... Moth-er... Moth-er, come with me. I want to be sure that you see what I see.

The Mother *(raising herself on her elbow)*

What is the mat-ter with you now? What is all this fuss a - bout?_____ Who is it then?

Amahl

(hesitatingly)

Moth-er... out - side the door there is... there is a King with a crown.

The Mother

51

Allegro

(Still bowing, the Mother makes way for the Kings to enter, pulling Amahl with her. The Page enters first, places his

52

lantern on the stool beside the fireplace, and drops his bundles. Almost immediately, King Kaspar proceeds at a stately march to

53

take his place on the bench, stage right. The Page hurries to hold King Kaspar's train. Once Kaspar has placed himself, Balthazar

54

enters and proceeds to a place beside him. Melchior is the last to take his place. The Page runs back and forth to carry the

train of each. Amahl watches the procession with growing wonder and excitement.)

55

* The step of the march of the Kings should fall on the first and third beats of the music.

When the Three Kings are together, they sit as one. The Page spreads the rug before them and sets upon it the gifts
Kings bear for the Ch

The Mother

(The Mothe

Adagio

Mother: I shall go and gath-er wood for the fire.   I've noth-ing in the house.

Melchior

Melchior: It is nice here.   We ca

Adagio

Amahl **(whispering to his mother)**

Amahl: What did I tell you?

takes her shawl from the peg and goes to the door.)

Mother: Your star?   Sh!

Melchior: on - ly stay a lit-tle while.   We must not   lose sight of our star.   We

Amahl: No, Moth-e

Mother: I shall be right back... and A-mahl, don't be a nui-sance. *quickly*

(She goe

Melchior: still have a long way to go.

24

28

King, as King he was born. But no one will bring him in-cense or gold, though sick and

poor and hun-gry and cold. He's my child, my son, my dar-ling, my own.

rit.

p

rit.

a tempo

Have you seen a Child the col-or of earth, the col-or of thorn? His

Have you seen a Child the col-or of earth, the col-or of thorn? His

p a tempo

eyes are sad, His hands are those of the poor, as poor He was born.

eyes are sad, His hands are those of the poor, as poor He was born.

(The calls of the shepherds fall sharp and clear on the air, breaking the hushed silence of the room. The Mother looks instinctively to see if her room is ready to receive her neighbors, then she goes to the door and opens it wide.)

(First singly, then in twos and threes, the shepherds begin to appear. They come from all directions. On the hills in the distance lantern lights pierce the darkness. Slowly they converge and move down the road toward the hut, led by a radiant Amahl.)

Allegretto, con grazia

34

(Ragged and joyous,the shepherds approach the hut, bearing their baskets of fruit and vegetables.)

(The shepherds crowd together in the frame of the door of the hut, struck dumb by the sight of the Kings, not d
to enter. Amahl, however, slips through the crowd to take his place beside his mother.)

(Shy and embarrassed, everyone tries to push his neighbor in ahead of him, until all of them are crowde
into one corner of the room.)

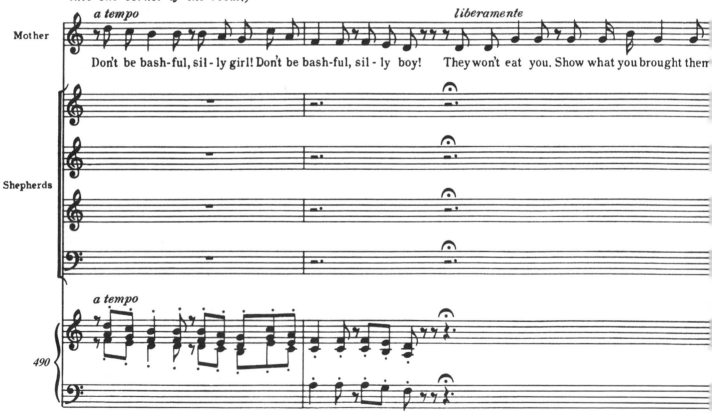

(*A second shepherd crosses to the Kings, presents his gifts, and returns, bowing, to his place.*)

40

42

(*The dance of the shepherds, which may include two or more dancers, should combine the qualities of prim- folk dancing and folk ritual. It is both an entertainment and a ceremony of welcome and hospitality. The d- ers are at first shy and fearful at the realization that they are in the presence of three great Kings, and th- movements are at times faltering and hesitant. But from the "Allegro vivace" on, the dance should assume the acter of a tarantella, gaining in pace and sureness and ending in a joyous frenzy.*)

43

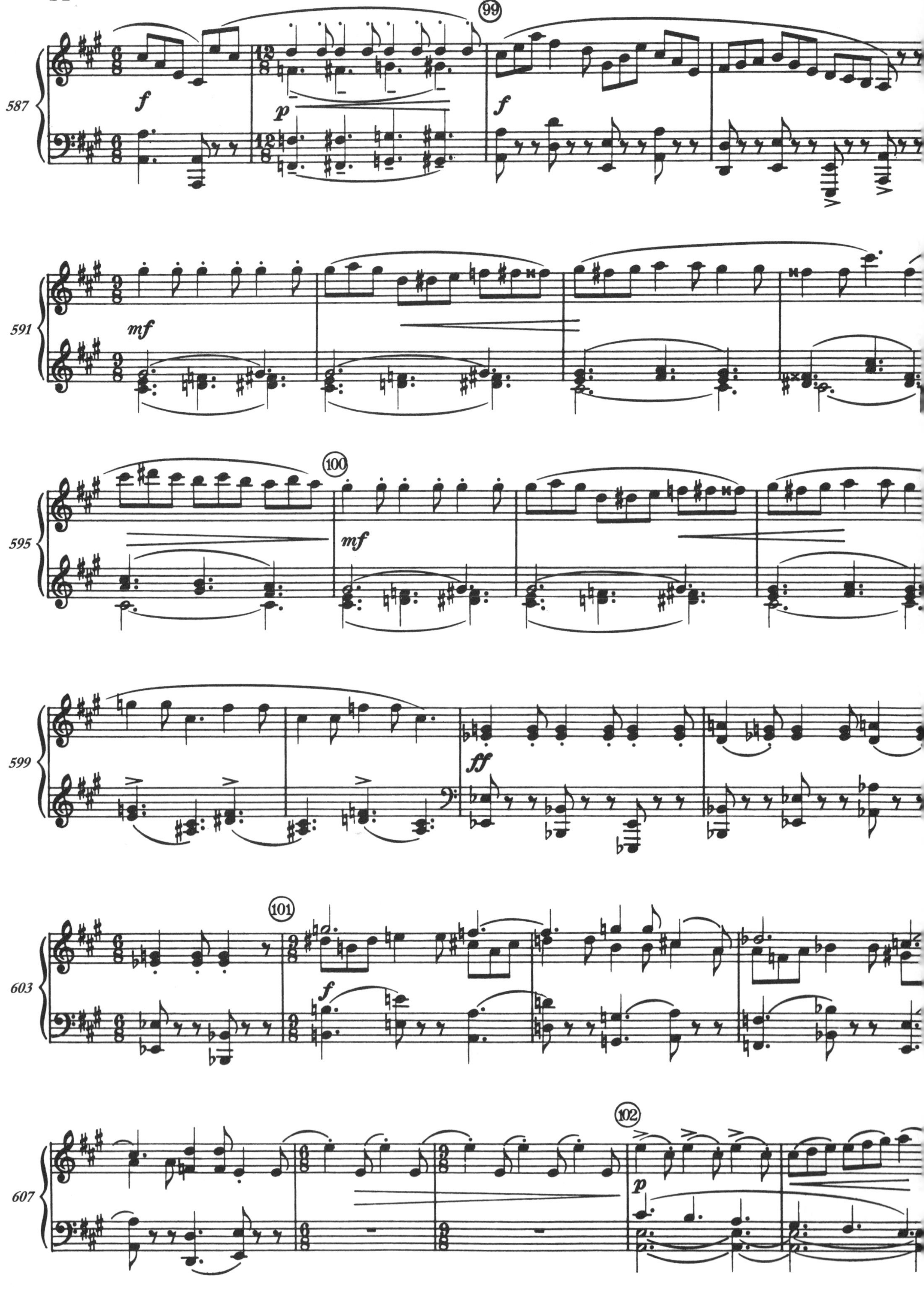

587
f
p
99
591
mf
595
100
599
ff
603
101
607
102

(Balthazar rises to thank the dancers, then resumes his seat.)

liberamente

Thank you, good friends, for your danc - es and your gifts. But now we must bid you good night. We have lit - tle time for sleep and a long jour - ney a - head.

(The shepherds pass before the Kings, bowing as they depart. The Mother bids them good night at the door and for a moment watches them down the road. After all have gone their voices are still heard on the winter air.)

Adagio, ma non troppo

Good night, my good Kings, good night and fare - well. The pale stars fore-tell that dawn is in

Good night, my good Kings, good night and fare - well. The pale stars fore-tell that dawn is in

Good night, my good Kings, good night and fare - well. The pale stars fore-tell that dawn is in

Good night, my good Kings, good night and fare - well. The pale stars fore-tell that dawn is in

(Amahl makes a gesture as if about to repeat his question; then, feeling defeated by Kaspar's deafness, gives up and walks sadly to his pallet of straw.)

Nev - er mind . . . good night.

Eh?

ppp

Good night, good night. The dawn is in

ppp

Good night, good night. The dawn is in

ppp

Good night, good night. The

ppp

Good night, good night. The

Andante sostenuto

(The Mother and Amahl have lain down on their pallets. The Kings, still sitting on the rude bench, settle themselves to sleep, leaning against each other. The Page curls himself up at their feet, his arms laid protectively over the rich gifts. His lantern has been placed on the floor by the fireplace, leaving only a dim glow in the room.)

sight. Good night, fare-well, good night, good night.

sight. Good night, fare-well, good night, good night.

day will be bright. Good night, fare-well, good night.

day will be bright. Good night, fare-well, good night.

Andante sostenuto

p dolcissimo

(During the interlude the lights in the hut should be lowered completely to denote the passage of time. On the last chords of the interlude the interior of the hut is slowly lighted by the first pale rays of the dawn from the hills.)

(112) *(Still sitting on her pallet, the Mother cannot take her eyes from the treasure guarded by the Page.)*

Mother: All that gold! All that gold! I won-der if rich peo-ple know what to do with their

Mother: gold! Do they know how____ a child____could be fed? Do rich peopl

Mother: know? Do they know that a house can be kept warm all day with burn-ing logs? Do rich peo-p

52

54

bash in your head! Don't you dare! Don't you dare! Don't you dare, ug-ly man, hurt my

moth - er! Don't you dare! Don't you dare! Don't you dare!

(At a sign from Kaspar, the Page releases the Mother. Still kneeling, she raises her arms toward her son. Choked by tears, Amahl staggers toward her and, letting his crutch fall, collapses, sobbing, into his mother's arms.)

Oh, wo - man, you may keep the

gold. The Child we seek ___ does-n't need our gold. On love, on love a-lone ___

___ He will build His King-dom. His pierc-ed hand will hold no scep-ter. His ha-loed head will wear no

Melchior: crown. His might will not be built on your toil. Swift-er than light-ni

Melchior: He will soon walk a-mong us. He will bring us new life—and re-ceive our death, and the keys to Hi

(turning to the other Kings)

Melchior: cit - y be-long to the poor._____ Let us leave, my friends.

(Freeing herself from Amahl's embrace, the Mother throws herself on her knees before the Kings, spilling the
she has taken from her hands onto the carpet. Meanwhile, Amahl is on his feet, leaning on his crutch.)

Mother: *very slowly and deliberately* Oh, no, wait . . . take back your gold! *lento, espressivo* For such a King I've wait - ed___ all my life. And if I were-n't

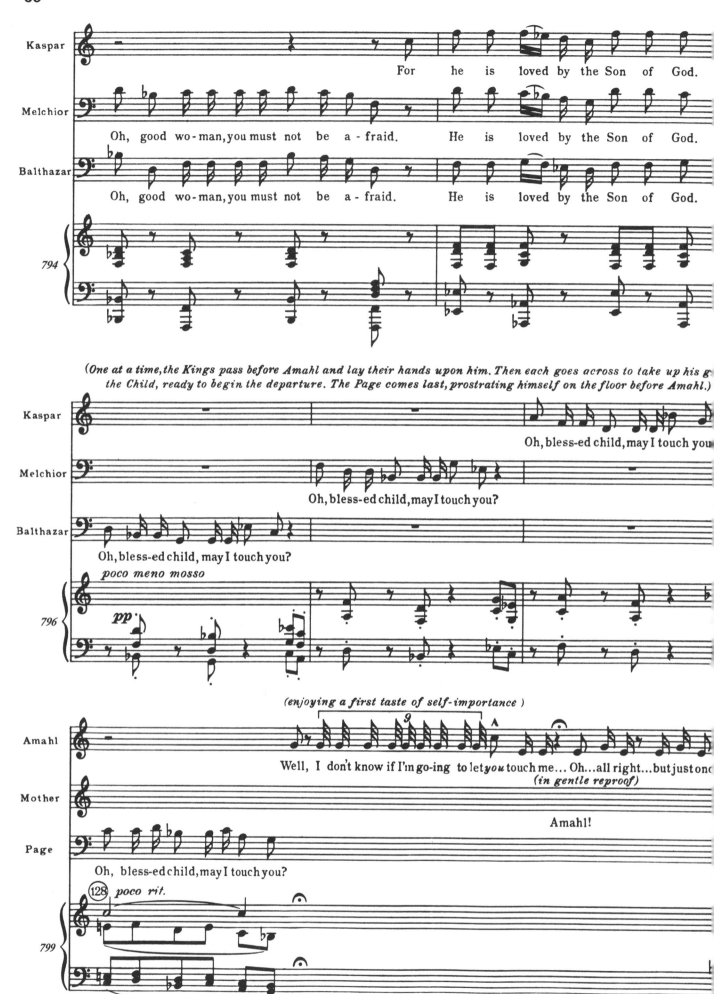

62

(Having taken his place at the end of the procession, Amahl begins to play his pipes as he goes. Outside, the soft colors of dawn are brightening the sky, and a few great flakes of snow have begun to fall upon the road.)

(The Mother stands alone in the

Allegro ma non troppo

Allegro ma non troppo

doorway of the cottage. Then she goes outside to wave once more to Amahl, as he turns to her, just before he

disappears at the bend in the road.)

poco meno

dolce

espr.

(The curtain falls very slowly.)

Fine